Festivals
and Feasts

Contents

Features

Holiday might be one of your favorite words, but do you know where it came from? Learn more on page 5.

Discover a treasure of wartime memories in an old family album. Turn to **The War Years** on page 23 for more.

Read one boy's scrapbook and join in the fun when a small town gets together to race homemade cars in **Apple Box Derby Day** on page 25.

Study this calendar to find a world of festivals and feasts so you can be the first to wish a faraway friend happy holidays. See page 28.

What age-old festival is called "Fat Tuesday" in French?

Visit www.rigbyinfoquest.com
for more about FESTIVALS.

Feasts, Fireworks, and Fancy Dress

On almost every day of the year, there is a festival or a feast taking place somewhere. People all over the world get together with family and friends to celebrate special days of the year and special times in their lives. They prepare fancy foods and dress in fine clothes. They often take part in parades and dance in the streets. Most festivals are colorful, noisy, and happy. Many have been celebrated in the same way for hundreds of years.

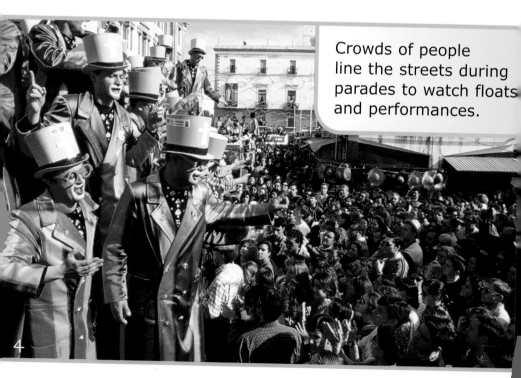

Crowds of people line the streets during parades to watch floats and performances.

Many festivals honor special days in the history of a nation. Cinco de Mayo is a holiday in Mexico.

WORD BUILDER

Holidays are special days in the year when people do not have to go to work or school. The word *holiday* comes from an Old English word meaning "holy day." It is a day when people have time off to celebrate a special event. Every country has its own holidays.

5

Celebrating Seasons

Spring Fever

People have always celebrated the changing seasons. Spring festivals are usually full of bright, spring-flower colors. Many countries around the world hold spring festivals. Holi is a spring festival in India that celebrates the arrival of spring flowers. It is known as the festival of color. Painted elephants lead great processions of dancers down the streets. During Holi, people throw colored water over one another.

Easter is a special holiday time that falls during spring in many parts of the world. In so countries, people line the streets with beautiful flower-petal carpets for the Easter celebration

Summary Fun

Notting Hill Carnival is one of the world's most famous summer street festivals. This huge party in the street is held each year in London, England. People work hard to create wild costumes to wear to the carnival. They often paint their faces, and many dance to the rhythm and beat of steel drums. Storytellers entertain people by singing funny story poems called calypsos. More than one million people go to the Notting Hill Carnival each year.

England

The Caribbean

London is a city full of people from many countries and backgrounds. People from the Caribbean first began the Notting Hill Carnival to keep the sights and sounds of their faraway lands alive in their new home.

9

Harvest Holidays

The harvesting of crops has long been a cause for festivals and feasts. Thanksgiving is a traditional harvest holiday celebrated by people in Canada and the United States. It is a time when families gather to share a special meal and to give thanks for the good things in their lives.

Kwanzaa is a harvest festival celebrated each year by African Americans. It is a time for people to remember their culture and their African **heritage**. During Kwanzaa, families set up displays of fruit and vegetables and communities often feast together. People dress in traditional African clothing. They perform plays, make speeches, and give small gifts.

The first Thanksgiving feast was held by the Pilgrims who came to North America to start a new life. It was only because of the friendship of a local American Indian that the newcomers had a big enough harvest to last the winter. To show their thanks, the Pilgrims held a festival for the Indians. For three days, they feasted, played games, and told stories together.

The number seven is very important in many African cultures. During Kwanzaa, families light seven candles.

Winter Wonder

The lights and colors of a festival and the warmth and friendship of a feast are good ways to brighten the darkest days of the year. Many countries celebrate winter with special **customs** and carnivals. During Kamakura, a snow festival in Japan, people build snow caves. Children dress warmly and play games in their snow caves. They often have a supply of apples and nuts to offer visitors.

Kamakura

In many cold northern countries, winter nights come alive with the magic of ice sculpture. During winter carnivals, people can walk through huge castles made from blocks of ice. Life-sized ice sculptures line the streets. The ice art is lit with bright lights to create a winter wonderland.

Japan

Many people come to the snow festivals held in Japan during February. Children enjoy racing down ice slides in the city of Sapporo during the festival there.

New Beginnings

Long ago, people believed that bright lights and loud noises would scare away bad luck. In many countries, people use fireworks, lanterns, candles, and colored lights to bring in a new year.

New Year is the most important Chinese festival. For two weeks, people celebrate with family, friends, feasts, and fun. Acrobats, jugglers, and musicians perform in the streets. During the Dragon Parade, dancers crouch, spin, and leap beneath huge dragons made of paper or silk.

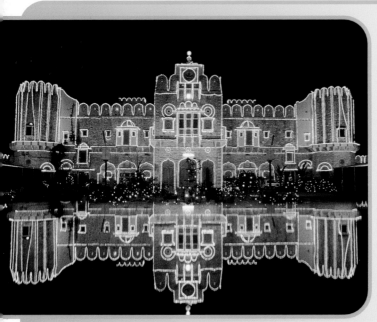

In India, many people celebrate a new year with a festival of lights called Diwali. Buildings are lit with row after row of colored lights. Many people believe that lights show the way for good luck in the new year.

China

The Lantern Festival ends the Chinese New Year celebrations. Lanterns are made of paper, glass, or silk. They are often bright red. Red is a lucky color during Chinese New Year.

Nation Celebration

People often gather to celebrate their history and their way of life. For many American Indians and Canadian Indians, a powwow is the most important cultural event of the year. Powwows are held across North America all year round. Each one lasts for three days. During a powwow, tribes gather to celebrate their culture and traditions.

Children often compete in traditional dances during a powwow. They learn from their elders and dress in tribal costumes for these happy times.

Through story dances, songs, and the sharing of time with family and friends, powwows are a powerful way of keeping traditional ceremonies, languages, and customs alive.

Family and Friends

A wedding is a special time when friends and family gather to celebrate the beginning of a new family.

People all around the world follow many different customs and traditions during a wedding **ceremony**. In many cultures, a bride and a groom exchange special promises called vows. For this, they dress in their finest clothes. They often share a feast and a wedding cake with their guests. Many guests give gifts to help the couple as they set out on their new life together.

It is a tradition in many weddings for the father of the bride to walk his daughter down the aisle. Close friends and family of the bride and groom often play a special part in a wedding. A little sister may be a flower girl, for example, and a young nephew a ring bearer.

Growing Up

There are many festivals and feasts just for children. These often mark growing-up times in a child's life. They are a sign of change. In the Cook Islands, for example, the cutting of a boy's hair for the very first time signals that he has left boyhood behind and become a young man. Family and friends gather from near and far for this special occasion.

To begin, the boy has his hair tied in long ribbons. As each guest greets the boy, they give him a gift of money and snip off a lock of hair. The ceremony ends with a feast, speeches, and dancing. In the eyes of his family, the boy has now become a young man.

A Day to Remember

Many countries around the world set aside special days to remember the soldiers who fought for freedom during the wars of the last century. Many of those soldiers died fighting. Some live on today as grandparents or great grandparents, but they take time on special days of the year to remember past friends and brave battles.

During **memorial** days, people make speeches and hold special ceremonies. Many people wear paper poppies as a **symbol** of the war days. These blood-red flowers grew on some battlefields.

Australia

New Zealand

ANZAC Day is celebrated on April 25 in Australia and New Zealand. It began in honor of troops who fought in World War I and now honors all soldiers. ANZAC stands for Australia and New Zealand Army Corps.

The War Years

Here is my grandpa, Sergeant John Thomson, as a young soldier in the New Zealand Medical Corps, 1942.

Safely Back From Italian Prison Camps

A group of New Zealanders photographed at the base camp in the Middle East when they returned. These men, who were prisoners, were given their freedom in exchange for Italians, and most of them severely wounded or medical personnel.

Grandpa and his twin brother were held as prisoners of war in the very same POW camp. Imagine how they felt when they bumped into each other there!

SOLDIER'S SERVICE AND PAY BOOK

23

Small Town Fun

Sometimes small towns hold festivals of their own. Schools, clubs, and community groups often take part in races and special events. Many town festiva date back to grandparents' times. Over the years, it becomes a tradition for a whole town to get together for a day of fun, food, and races.

On fair days, there are often food stalls, games, and fun contests.

Apple Box Derby Day

I will never forget this day! I raced in the Apple Box Derby. Derby day is a big day in our town. This was my very first time to race. It all began when Grandpa built me my own racing car. He painted it apple green, and I love it!

Grandpa and me (Seth!)

Wow, Grandpa, you're the greatest!

On race day, we had to weigh in. Then my car was lifted onto the starting ramp next to another car, and it was time to race... 3, 2, 1, GO!

We zoomed off. During my first race, I spun out and lost a wheel! Luckily someone loaned me another one and I was soon racing again. I won my second race! My family and friends shouted and cheered. It was so COOL!

25

Holidays and History

Many holidays date back to ancient times, and the symbols that people used long ago are used to this day. Symbols bring special meaning to a holiday celebration. Do you know the meaning behind some of the symbols we often use today?

In medieval times, May Day was a favorite holid in English villages. The first of May is the start of spring. People still enj dancing around a maypo hung with bright ribbons

What age-old festival is called "Fat Tuesday" in French?

Visit **www.rigbyinfoquest.com**
for more about FESTIVALS.

The Christmas Tree – In many countries, Christmas falls in winter. For hundreds of years, people have decorated evergreen trees with bright lights and colorful ornaments as a reminder of life during the winter darkness.

The Easter Egg – In many countries, Easter falls in spring, when new plants grow and animal babies are born. It is a custom to give eggs during Easter because eggs are a symbol of new life. Flowers are also a symbol of Easter.

The Jack-o'-Lantern – People often carve scary faces in pumpkins for Halloween. Jack-o'-lanterns are named after a naughty boy called Jack who was always playing tricks. Wearing Halloween costumes and going trick-or-treating are Halloween customs.

The Hanukkiyah – Also called the menorah, this is the most important symbol of Hanukkah, the Jewish light festival. There are eight days of Hanukkah, and a candle is lit for each day. During Hanukkah, families feast, sing songs, and play games.

Valentine Hearts – People have celebrated Valentine's Day for hundreds of years. They often send cards decorated with hearts to their loved ones. Long ago, people thought their feelings came from their hearts, so the heart became a symbol of love.

27

FACT FINDER

Look closely at this calendar of festivals:

· What festivals can you find and name?
· What festivals does your family celebrate?
· What festivals do you think are celebrated in other countries?

Turn to page 30 for the answers.

A Calendar of Festivals

1 New Year's Day: Jan 1
2 Australia Day: Jan 26
3 Chinese New Year: Jan to Feb*
4 Kamakura Snow Festival: Feb*
5 Holi: Feb to Mar*
6 Valentine's Day: Feb 14
7 Mardi Gras: Feb to Mar*
8 Japan Doll Festival: Mar 3
9 Easter: Mar to Apr*
10 Earth Day: Apr 22
11 ANZAC Day: Apr 25
12 May Day: May 1
13 Memorial Day: May*
14 Cinco de Mayo: May 5
15 Dragon Boat Festival: Jun*
16 Canada Day: Jul 1

17 Independence Day: Jul 4
18 Bastille Day: Jul 14
19 Notting Hill Carnival: Aug*
20 Rosh Hashana: Sep*
21 Labor Day: Sep*
22 Thanksgiving (Canada) Oct*
23 Diwali: Oct 31
24 Halloween: Oct 31
25 Day of the Dead: Nov 1
26 Guy Fawkes: Nov 5
27 Veteran's Day: Nov 11
28 Thanksgiving (U.S.A.): Nov
29 Hanukkah: Dec*
30 Christmas: Dec 25
31 Kwanzaa: Dec 26
✦ These festivals fall on slight
different dates each year.

Glossary

ceremony – formal actions and words performed during a special occasion, such as a wedding

custom – something that is followed as a tradition through time in a family, a culture, or a country

heritage – valuable and important traditions that are handed down from older people to younger people

memorial – a special time or place that helps people remember people or events of the past

symbol – an object that stands for something else and makes people think of another meaning

Index

Discussion Starters

1 No matter where they live,
people celebrate special times of
the year and special days in their lives.
In what ways are the festivals in this
book similar? How are they different?

2 Choose a festival that you are not very
familiar with from pages 28–29. How could
you find out more about the customs and
traditions behind this festival?

3 In Italy, the song of a cricket is a sign
of spring. During Italy's Cricket Festival,
street stalls sell chirping crickets in bright
cages, and families gather for a holiday.
They say that if the crickets still chirp
when the children go to bed, they will
have a year of good luck! What fun
festival can you make up to mark
the beginning of a new season?